THE DRIVERS OF EMPLOYEE ENGAGEMENT

Other titles from IES:

New Reward I: Team, Skill and Competency Based Pay
Reilly P (Ed.)
IES Report 403, 2003. ISBN 1 85184 330 9

e-Recruitment: Is it Delivering?
Kerrin M, Kettley P
IES Report 402, 2003. ISBN 1 85184 329 9

Measuring Up: Benchmarking Graduate Retention
Tyers C, Perryman S, Barber L
IES Report 401, 2003. ISBN 1 85184 328 0

Your Graduates and You:
Effective Strategies for Graduate Recruitment and Development
Connor H, Hirsh W, Barber L
IES Report 400, 2003. ISBN 1 85184 327 2

eHR: An Introduction
Kettley P, Reilly P
IES Report 398, 2003. ISBN 1 85184 326 4

Kirkpatrick and Beyond: A review of models of training evaluation
Tamkin P, Yarnall J, Kerrin M
IES Report 392, 2002. ISBN 1 85184 321 3

Resourcing the Training and Development Function
Carter A, Hirsh W, Aston J
IES Report 390, 2002. ISBN 1 85184 319 1

Chore to Champions: the making of better people managers
Tamkin P, Hirsh W, Tyers C
IES Report 389, 2003. ISBN 1 85184 318 3

New Directions in Management Development
Hirsh W, Carter A
IES Report 387, 2002. ISBN 1 85184 316 7

A catalogue of these and over 100 other titles is available from IES,
or on the IES Website, www.employment-studies.co.uk

The Drivers of Employee Engagement

Dilys Robinson
Sarah Perryman
Sue Hayday

IES Research Networks

Report 408

Published by:

INSTITUTE FOR EMPLOYMENT STUDIES
Mantell Building
Falmer
Brighton BN1 9RF
UK

Tel.   + 44 (0) 1273 686751
Fax   + 44 (0) 1273 690430

http://www.employment-studies.co.uk

British Cataloguing-in-Publication Data

A catalogue record for this publication is available from the British Library

ISBN 1 85184 336 1

Printed and bound by Antony Rowe Ltd, Eastbourne

The Institute for Employment Studies

IES is an independent, international and apolitical centre of research and consultancy in human resource issues. It works closely with employers in the manufacturing, service and public sectors, government departments, agencies, and professional and employee bodies. For over 30 years the Institute has been a focus of knowledge and practical experience in employment and training policy, the operation of labour markets and human resource planning and development. IES is a not-for-profit organisation which has over 60 multidisciplinary staff and international associates. IES expertise is available to all organisations through research, consultancy, publications and the Internet.

IES aims to help bring about sustainable improvements in employment policy and human resource management. IES achieves this by increasing the understanding and improving the practice of key decision makers in policy bodies and employing organisations.

The IES Research Networks

This report is the product of a study supported by the IES Research Networks, through which Members finance, and often participate in, applied research on employment issues. Full information on Membership is available from IES on request, or at www.employment-studies.co.uk/networks/

Acknowledgements

The authors would like to thank their colleagues at IES:

Helen Wolfe for putting together the Royal Bank of Scotland case study.

Michael Silverman for the commitment literature review.

Rob Barkworth for the organisational citizenship behaviour review.

Hülya Hooker for assisting with the analysis.

Carol Barber for report production.

Vic Hartley for his peer review.

Contents

Executive Summary

What is engagement?

IES' first research step was to investigate what HR professionals understood when they used the term 'engagement'. A clear view of the behaviours demonstrated by the engaged employee emerged:

- belief in the organisation
- desire to work to make things better
- understanding of business context and the 'bigger picture'
- respectful of, and helpful to, colleagues
- willingness to 'go the extra mile'
- keeping up-to-date with developments in the field.

Engagement has clear overlaps with the more exhaustively researched concepts of commitment and organisational citizenship behaviour, but there are also differences. In particular, engagement is two-way; organisations must work to engage the employee, who in turn has a choice about the level of engagement to offer the employer.

IES defines engagement as 'a positive attitude held by the employee towards the organisation and its values. An engaged employee is aware of business context, and works with colleagues to improve performance within the job for the benefit of the organisation. The organisation must work to develop and nurture engagement, which requires a two-way relationship between employer and employee.'

Measuring engagement

Our analysis used data from IES' 2003 attitude survey of over 10,000 employees in 14 organisations in the NHS. Twelve attitude statements representing engagement were tested; all 12 were found to 'sit together' reliably, to comprise a single indicator of engagement. Although tested within the NHS, the statements are not NHS-specific; they can be transferred to other organisations and sectors. If attitude survey space is at a premium, and organisations feel unable to include 12 statements, an engagement sub-set of five statements can be used instead. This sub-set can be safely used, as it represents the essence of engagement and has been tested for reliability.

Positive responses to the engagement statements indicate:

- a positive attitude towards, and pride in, the organisation
- belief in the organisations' products/services
- a perception that the organisation enables the employee to perform well
- a willingness to behave altruistically and be a good team-player
- an understanding of the bigger picture and a willingness to go beyond the requirements of the job.

Engagement challenges

Further in-depth analysis of our NHS case-study data revealed that engagement levels can vary, in association with a variety of personal and job characteristics and with experiences at work. Some key findings were:

- engagement levels decline as employees get older — until they reach the oldest group (60 plus), where levels suddenly rise, and show this oldest group to be the most engaged of all
- minority ethnic respondents have higher engagement levels than their white colleagues
- managers and professionals tend to have higher engagement levels than their colleagues in supporting roles, although people in the latter group appear to owe greater loyalty to their profession than to the organisation in which they practise their craft
- engagement levels decline as length of service increases

- having an accident or an injury at work, or experiencing harassment (particularly if the manager is the source of the harassment) both have a big negative impact on engagement

- employees who have a personal development plan, and who have received a formal performance appraisal within the past year, have significantly higher engagement levels than those who have not.

The above findings show that organisations need to work hard to prevent, and minimise the impact of, bad experiences. They also need to ensure that employees' development needs (including the special needs of professionals) are taken seriously; pay attention to, and value the roles of, support staff; and to maintain the interest of longer-serving employees. The relatively high levels of engagement of the oldest employees, and of minority ethnic staff, suggest sources of untapped potential within some organisations.

What drives engagement?

Research shows that committed employees perform better. If we accept that engagement, as many believe, is 'one-step up' from commitment, it is clearly in the organisation's interests to understand the drivers of engagement. Analysis of the NHS case study data indicates that opinions about, and experiences of, many aspects of working life are strongly correlated with engagement levels. However, the strongest driver of all is a sense of feeling valued and involved. This has several key components:

- involvement in decision-making
- the extent to which employees feel able to voice their ideas, and managers listen to these views, and value employees' contributions
- the opportunities employees have to develop their jobs
- the extent to which the organisation is concerned for employees' health and well-being.

The line manager clearly has a very important role in fostering employees' sense of involvement and value – an observation that is completely consistent with IES' research in many different areas of HR practice and employment, all of which point to the critical importance of the employee-manager relationship.

IES' diagnostic tool

The IES engagement model illustrates the strong link between feeling valued and involved and engagement. In addition to the model, IES offers a diagnostic tool that can be used to derive organisation-specific drivers from attitude survey data. Our findings suggest that many of the drivers of engagement will be common to all organisations, regardless of sector; however, some variability is likely, and the relative strength of each driver is also likely to be contingent upon the organisation being studied.

General lessons

Attempts to raise engagement levels are likely to founder, unless the following 'building blocks' are in place:

- good quality line management
- two-way communication
- effective internal co-operation
- a development focus
- commitment to employee well-being
- clear, accessible HR policies and practices, to which managers at all levels are committed.

It looks easy, but of course it isn't; it requires a huge amount of effort and continuing investment to ensure that all of these basics are in place and working well. Embarking on a drive to increase engagement levels should not be undertaken lightly, bearing in mind the ease with which engagement (like the psychological contract) can be shattered.

The study

IES' research into employee engagement was promoted by the interest and involvement of several Member companies. It proved more complicated than first envisaged, due to the lack of existing research in the area. IES explored the concept of engagement with member and client organisations, before embarking on original research into measuring engagement and establishing its main drivers. The database used for the research comprises 2003 attitude survey data from 14 organisations in the

NHS (10,024 completed questionnaires). The full range of employee groups and job roles were represented — managerial, professional, technical and support (manual and administrative).

This report also contains literature reviews on commitment and organisational citizenship behaviour, and a Royal Bank of Scotland case study.

The study was funded and supported by IES' motivation, well-being and retention research network.

1. Introduction

1.1 Why engagement?

This research described in this report was prompted by our contact with several large, private-sector companies, all of who spoke with considerable enthusiasm about the engagement models they were in the process of adopting. It appeared that engagement elicited more empathy and enthusiasm and was, intuitively, better understood than the associated concept of commitment.

With the knowledge that HR people in leading-edge companies were 'engaging with engagement', IES researchers felt that it would be an appropriate concept to investigate, understand and evaluate on behalf of our member organisations. Specifically:

● what is engagement?

● does it differ from commitment, or is it an old concept repackaged?

● can it be measured?

● how does an engaged employee behave, and does this bring organisational benefits?

● are these engaged behaviours similar to those described by researchers in organisational citizenship behaviour, or is there a difference?

● if there are benefits to be had, how can engagement be nurtured and grown?

For such a well-used and popular term, engagement has surprisingly little associated research. In fact, a trawl of the literature revealed only a handful of studies, although several references were uncovered relating to models and methods of analysis promoted by consultancies and survey houses, and their use by large companies.

1.2 Approach and methodology

Given the lack of academic research and the limited amount of empirical evidence available, IES embarked on an original piece of research under the auspices of its 'motivation, well-being and retention' Research Network. The aim of the study was to define engagement, devise a method of measuring it, and establish its drivers — that is, the other aspects of working life which influence it most strongly.

The following methodology was adopted:

- a literature search to uncover references to engagement and the closely related concepts of commitment and organisational citizenship behaviour

- discussions with IES member companies about their understanding of engagement and its business benefits.

- development of engagement attitude statements for use in employee attitude surveys

- testing of the statements in attitude surveys run on behalf of the NHS in the period January to July 2003

- development and testing of an engagement indicator from the attitude statements

- use of the indicator in further analysis, to establish differences in engagement levels by employee group — using variables related to respondents' biographical and job variables, and also their experiences at work

- further statistical analysis of the survey data to identify other aspects of working life that impact most strongly on engagement, and could be seen as drivers.

1.3 Report contents

The structure of this report is as follows:

Chapter 2 discusses engagement as a concept, compares it to commitment and organisational citizenship behaviour, and establishes a definition.

Chapter 3 focuses on the reasons why organisations should pay attention to employees' engagement levels, specifically the potential business benefits.

Chapter 4 describes how engagement can be measured and analysed.

Chapter 5 discusses the drivers of engagement and the IES engagement model.

Chapter 6 contains conclusions, recommendations and suggestions for further research.

2. What is Engagement?

2.1 The facets of engagement

2.1.1 Engagement choices

The verb 'to engage' has a variety of meanings, ranging from straightforward and transactional (to hire someone to do a job), to exciting and mysterious (to fascinate and charm). Arranging these meanings in order, depending on the likely effort involved (see Figure 2.1) implies that organisations have a choice when it comes to engaging employees. They can choose the type of engagement they would like to offer, and the extent to which they go beyond the merely transactional – that is, how much effort they make to go towards the right-hand side of the diagram.

Employees, too, have a choice. They can choose, in the first place, whether or not to be attracted into the organisation – and, having arrived, they can decide whether or not their job continues to interest them sufficiently to stay in it and develop it. Some employees rarely move beyond a transactional relationship, but many require something more from their jobs – a sense of self-worth and of being valued, and an opportunity

Figure 2.1: The engagement effort

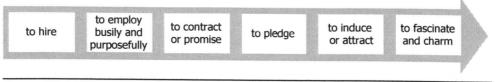

Source: IES, 2003

Institute for Employment Studies

to succeed and progress. Those aspects of a job that engage a particular employee may vary over his or her working lifetime, in line with changing circumstances and interests.

2.1.2 The HR view

IES' HR contacts, in companies known to have already adopted employee engagement models, or to be in the process of considering doing so, have a variety of views about how to define engagement.

- Some emphasise the similarity of engagement to the psychological contract, in that it is unwritten, underpinned by trust, a two-way relationship between employer and employee — and easy to break.

- Others stress the need for engaged employees to identify with the organisation — to believe in its products or services, and particularly its values. This view indicates that engagement needs to be at a level that is beyond the job itself, embracing the whole organisation and what it stands for.

- Finally, another strand of opinion highlights the need for engaged employees to understand the context in which the organisation operates. It is insufficient for employees to be committed to their organisation; they also need an element of business appreciation, so that any changes they make to their jobs could be seen to have business benefits.

IES' HR contacts, when consulted during 2003, had clear and reasonably consistent views about the ways in which an engaged employee behaves (these are presented in a summary diagram in Figure 2.2, over). Although an organisation full of such employees would, without doubt, be every Chief Executive's dream, the two-way nature of engagement should be not forgotten. Organisations have to work to engage employees to this extent, and may have to put in a lot to reach their goal of a committed, enthusiastic, and engaged workforce — the achievement of which should not be undertaken lightly or half-heartedly.

2.2 Is engagement really new?

Engagement has similarities to, and overlaps with, two concepts that have academic pedigrees and have been the subjects of

Source: IES, 2003

empirical research — commitment and organisational citizenship behaviour (OCB). This short section firstly describes the results of the engagement literature review (which revealed very little), then outlines the similarities and differences between these themes and the concept of engagement. Readers who are interested in reading more about commitment and OCB can find literature reviews in Appendix 1 (Commitment) and Appendix 2 (OCB).

2.2.1 Engagement references

Despite the apparent importance of engagement, relatively little academic research has been conducted in this area. Most of the references relate to work done by survey houses and consultancies. For example Hewitt, Bacon and Woodrow,[1] have defined engagement as *'the measure of an employee's emotional and intellectual commitment to their organisation and its success'* and believe it to be an outcome measure, as it describes how

---

[1]   Formerly Hewitt Associates

employees behave as a result of their interactions with the organisation. In addition, engagement is seen as going beyond job satisfaction, referring to an employee's personal state of involvement, contribution, and ownership.

One study (Harter *et al.*, 2002) found that both employee satisfaction and engagement have a direct relationship to business outcomes. Their research involved 36 organisations, from a variety of public and private sector areas, and sought to examine the relationship between employee satisfaction, engagement and business unit outcomes. These included customer satisfaction, productivity, profit, employee turnover, and workplace accidents. Harter *et al.* (2002) defined engagement as referring to an individual's involvement and satisfaction with, as well as enthusiasm for, their work. This was based on Kahn's view (1990), that engagement occurs when:

> '... *individuals are emotionally connected to other, and are cognitively vigilant in their work.*'

Initial findings in this study indicated that engaged employees deliver better customer satisfaction; in addition, customer loyalty ratings improve and financial out-turn is better. There is also a relationship with employee turnover; as engagement increases, turnover decreases.

2.2.2 Commitment

Employee commitment is recognised as a contributor to business success, notably as a result of the work done by Sears in the USA. The 'service-profit chain' emphasises the importance of employee commitment to customer service, which in turn impacts on customer satisfaction and financial out-turn. IES' research in this area is described in Chapter 3 of this report.

A cursory examination of the concept, however, reveals that there are several different types of commitment, some of which have more in common with perceptions of engagement than others. These are described in more detail in Appendix 1. The closest relationship with engagement is the type of commitment known as 'affective'. This type of commitment emphasises the satisfaction people get from their jobs and their colleagues, and the willingness of employees to go beyond the call of duty for the good of the organisation. It also goes some way towards capturing the two-way nature of the engagement relationship, as employers are expected to provide a supportive working environment.

By contrast, the type of commitment with the least in common with engagement is 'structural' commitment. Employees with high levels of structural commitment view their relationship with their employer in a transactional way, *ie* they give their labour in return for a fair economic exchange. They are unlikely to leave due to barriers in the way of their exit (such as good working conditions, pensions, and generous pay rates). Such employees may express an intention to stay, only because there is no good reason to leave.

2.2.3 Organisational citizenship behaviour

OCB has attracted particular interest in recent years. It has several components, some of which align particularly well with engagement (see Appendix 2 for more information about OCB). OCB includes:

- helping behaviour
- sportsmanship
- organisational loyalty
- organisational compliance
- initiative
- civic virtue
- self-development.

Although the behaviours associated with the engaged employee have much in common with those demonstrated by the good organisational citizen, OCB is concerned with the characteristics and behaviour of the individual, rather than the organisation.

2.2.4 The verdict and the definition

Our analysis shows that engagement contains many of the elements of both commitment and OCB, but is by no means a perfect match with either. In addition, neither commitment nor OCB reflect sufficiently two aspects of engagement — its two-way nature, and the extent to which engaged employees are expected to have an element of business awareness.

IES offers the following definition:

'Engagement is a positive attitude held by the employee towards the organisation and its values. An engaged employee is aware of business context, and works with colleagues to improve performance within the job for the benefit of the organisation. The organisation must work to nurture, maintain and grow engagement, which requires a two-way relationship between employer and employee.'

3. Why Worry About Engagement?

3.1 Background to engagement

Earlier reference has been made to the extensive literature and research on employee commitment, and the evidence that increased levels of employee commitment are related to improved business performance. Given that commitment 'works', and the similarity of engagement to some aspects of commitment, it would seem to make intuitive sense that engagement also works to bring about business improvements. Some of the companies already using engagement models are beginning to see engagement as 'commitment plus' or 'one step up from commitment', so it is worth spending a little time to understand the relationship between commitment and business performance.

3.2 'From People to Profits'

IES research, in the UK retail sector, showed conclusively that employee commitment had a direct impact on sales. As well as the direct link (which was not expected at the start of the research), commitment influenced sales through improved customer loyalty and improved employee attendance. Broadly speaking, as employee commitment increased, sales went up; in addition, employee absence decreased, while customer satisfaction and customer spending intention increased, causing sales to go up even more. The relationship is illustrated in Figure 3.1.

The service-profit chain research carried out in the USA for Sears, and by IES for the retail sector in the UK, requires complex statistical modelling and uses data from different sources, all of which has to be closely matched. The majority of companies are

Figure 3.1: Service-profit chain

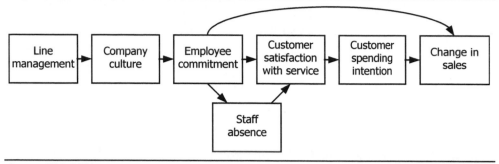

Source: IES, 2003

not in a position to carry out such time-consuming and difficult research, but there appears to be a general willingness to accept the underpinning finding: **the higher the level of employee commitment, the better the business outcome. If employee engagement is indeed one-step beyond commitment, the rewards should be even greater.**

3.3 Engagement at the Royal Bank of Scotland

The Royal Bank of Scotland (RBS) is a successful UK company that has the concept of employee engagement at the heart of its business strategy. The RBS model suggests that having employees who say they are **satisfied** with their jobs at RBS is only the starting point; as a next step, these employees should also be **committed** (that is, say they want to stay with the company). The ultimate goal is an **engaged** workforce, containing employees who are willing to make an extra effort to help the company achieve its goals (see Figure 3.2).

RBS used its extensive HR databases to develop an indicator to measure engagement, and now regularly assesses engagement levels via employee attitude surveys. Engagement is a fundamental plank of RBS' human capital reporting.

A case study describing RBS' approach to, and use of, engagement is in Appendix 3.

Figure 3.2: The RBS model of engagement

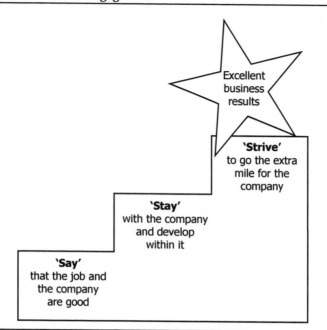

Excellent business results

'Strive' to go the extra mile for the company

'Stay' with the company and develop within it

'Say' that the job and the company are good

Source: *IES, 2003 adapted from the Royal Bank of Scotland and Hewitt Bacon and Woodrow*

4. Getting the Measure of Engagement

4.1 Approach

Measuring a concept such as engagement is challenging, as it involves attempting to assess complex feelings and emotions. The attitude survey is a useful tool for collecting, measuring and analysing employee opinions, although it can only be a blunt instrument, given the subtlety and nuances of shades of opinion. Nevertheless, it is a considerable improvement on the type of anecdotal evidence about employee morale on which decisions have sometimes been made. Having arrived at an understanding of organisations' views of the nature of engagement, and developed a definition, IES embarked on the process of developing and testing a series of attitudinal statements on the theme of engagement.

4.2 Engagement statements

4.2.1 Developing the statements

The IES engagement statements were developed with reference to a variety of sources:

- commitment statements already used by IES and other survey providers and researchers, and validated by frequent use in employee attitude surveys for employers in different sectors

- statements developed and validated by OCB researchers (see Appendix 2 for more detail about OCB research)

- statements relevant to the organisational context for the specific survey used for the testing and development of the engagement indicator.

4.2.2 The statements within the test environment

The 12 statements that were developed and tested are:

I speak highly of this organisation to my friends.

I would be happy for my friends and family to use this organisation's products/services.

This organisation is known as a good employer.

This organisation has a good reputation generally.

I am proud to tell others I am part of this organisation.

This organisation really inspires the very best in me in the way of job performance.

I find that my values and the organisation's are very similar.

I always do more than is actually required.

I try to help others in this organisation whenever I can.

I try to keep abreast of current developments in my area.

I volunteer to do things outside my job that contribute to the organisation's objectives.

I frequently make suggestions to improve the work of my team/ department/service.

The questionnaire containing the 12 engagement statements was administered to 14 organisations within the National Health Service (NHS). These organisations were NHS Trusts of different types — acute, teaching, and primary care. The smallest organisation contributed 46 completed questionnaires to the database, the largest 2,685. Altogether, the database in which the testing took place contains 10,024 cases. These include all major employee types — professional, support (manual and admini-strative), technical, and managerial.

The questionnaire used for testing the IES engagement statements collected a large amount of information about respondents — biographical, job-related, attitudes and experiences — that has been used to assess the extent to which engagement levels vary by employee group. It also assessed the extent to which engagement levels are influenced by the nature of the jobs employees do and their experiences at work.

Figure 4.1: Characteristics of an engaged employee, matched with engagement statements

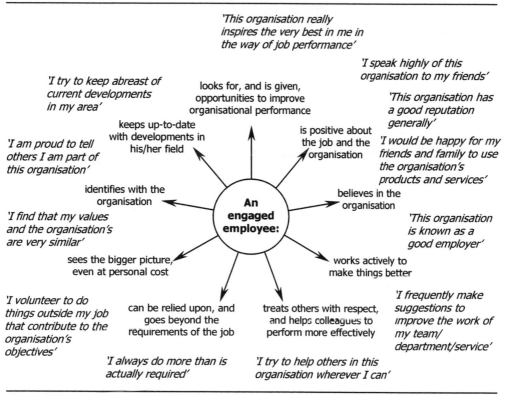

Source: IES

4.2.3 Match with the definition

Figure 4.1 relates the characteristics of an engaged employee (see Chapter 2 and Figure 2.2) to the engagement statements, and suggests that it is reasonably straightforward to map these statements onto general perceptions of what engagement is, and how an engaged employee behaves. The statements also go some way towards articulating the two-way nature of engagement, and the input that the organisation must make:

> *'This organisation really inspires the best in me in the way of job performance'* and *'This organisation is known as a good employer'*.

Underpinning several of the statements is a high level of personal motivation, which has been assumed, by participants in

IES' discussion with companies, to be a pre-requisite to engagement. This motivation has an altruistic feel to it, however; it is directed towards overall organisational improvement rather than to further the individual's own ends.

4.3 An indicator of engagement

4.3.1 The full indicator

IES carried out statistical tests to see if it would be valid to combine all 12 engagement statements into a single engagement indicator. The results were very encouraging (any statisticians reading this will be interested to hear that the alpha score was a high 0.86). This enabled IES to continue to analyse engagement levels, using an engagement indicator that comprises all 12 of the engagement statements listed in 4.2.2 above.

4.3.2 A condensed alternative

In many employee opinion surveys, space is at a premium. Competing issues jostle for attention, yet the longer the questionnaire, the less likely employees are to want to fill it in. Organisations wishing to measure engagement, but being unable to afford the luxury of including 12 statements, could consider statements based on the following sub-set:

- *I speak highly of this organisation to my friends* (implies a positive attitude and a pride in the organisation)
- *I would be happy for my friends and family to use this organisation's products/services* (suggests belief in the organisation and its outputs)
- *This organisation really inspires the very best in me in the way of job performance* (indicates that the individual feels enabled to do well, because the organisation is fulfilling its responsibilities in the two-way engagement relationship)
- *I try to help others in this organisation whenever I can* (shows a willingness to behave altruistically and be a good team-player)
- *I volunteer to do things outside my job that contribute to the organisation's objectives* (illustrates the employee's understanding of the bigger picture and willingness to 'go the extra mile').

4.4 Analysis using the engagement indicator

4.4.1 Approach to the analysis in the NHS

The engagement indicator can be used to give a single measure of engagement levels across the whole organisation. Its real power, however, lies in the ability it gives to organisations to compare one group with another, and to look at trends over time.

Within the NHS, the engagement indicator was used to see if engagement levels had any relationship with the following:

- biographical characteristics — gender, ethnicity, age group, having a disability/medical condition requiring support in the workplace, having caring responsibilities for children or an adult

- job characteristics — job group (for example, being a nurse, doctor, senior manager, technician *etc.*), length of service group, having a full/part-time contract, working pattern (shifts, rota, days)

- experiences at work — accidents, harassment, receiving a performance appraisal, having a personal development plan.

4.4.2 Results

Biographical characteristics

- The difference in engagement scores between men and women is not significant.

- Minority ethnic employees have higher engagement levels than their White colleagues. In addition, ethnic group makes a difference, with Black, Chinese and Asian employees having higher scores than those in Mixed and White groups. This finding would seem to support other research showing the business benefits of embracing diversity in the workplace.

- There are significant differences in scores when engagement levels are analysed by age group. In general, engagement levels go down slightly as employees get older — until they reach the oldest group, 60 and over, where the highest engagement levels of all are displayed. The high engagement levels expressed by experienced employees, who may be considered to be approaching the end of their working lives, suggests an untapped source of potential in many organisations.

- Further analysis indicates that employees in their 40s and 50s have the highest levels of workplace stress and are likely to find it difficult to balance work and home life — which suggests that attention to family friendly policies could increase the engagement levels of people in these age groups.

- The need for a family-friendly approach and greater emphasis on work-life balance is further underlined by the fact that employees with caring responsibilities for children have significantly lower engagement levels than those who have no caring responsibilities.

- Those with a disability/medical condition have lower engagement levels than those who do not have such a condition. This suggests that employers should look at the aspirations of employees with a disability — these employees perhaps feel that their potential is being overlooked and they have a lot more to offer.

Job characteristics

- Job group makes a big difference to engagement levels, as Figure 4.2 shows. In general, managers and professionals have higher levels of engagement than do their colleagues in supporting roles. However, the relatively low scores of doctors and midwives, and the relatively high scores of healthcare assistants, suggest that the relationship between job role and engagement is more complex than this broad statement would suggest.

- Working pattern and working hours make a difference to engagement level. Full-timers are significantly more engaged than part-timers, while employees who work days are more engaged than their colleagues on shifts or on a rota. This suggests that employers need to work harder with people who are not necessarily at work during 'standard' working times — to ensure that they receive communications, are managed effectively and have opportunities to grow and develop in their jobs.

- Figure 4.3 demonstrates that engagement levels go down as length of service increases — an indication to employers that they need to ensure that longer-serving employees continue to be exposed to new and interesting challenges.

Figure 4.2: Engagement levels by job group

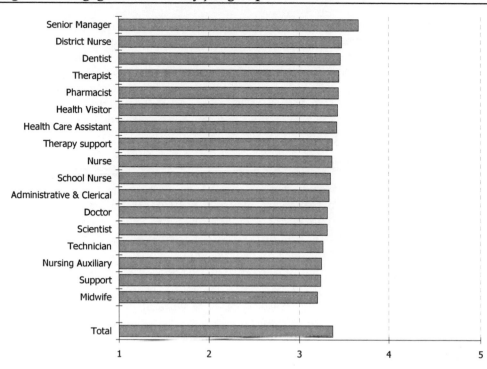

Source: IES, 2003

Figure 4.3: Engagement levels by length of service

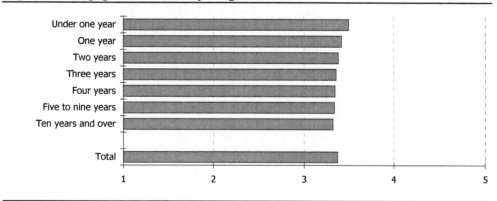

Source: IES, 2003

Experiences at work

- Having an accident or injury at work has a significant impact on engagement levels. Employees who have not had an accident or injury have relatively high engagement levels. Having one accident or injury is related to a reduction in this engagement score, while having between two and five accidents sees the score lowering further. This finding indicates the importance of accident prevention, and the need for good health and safety policies, practices and education.

- Exposure to harassment (verbal, racial or sexual) and/or violence in the workplace has a damaging impact on engagement. The source of the harassment is important. The impact of harassment from managers or colleagues is much greater than if the source is from patients or their relatives; the latter is often seen as an expected, if unpleasant, 'part of the job', while the former seems to be a big 'shock to the system'.

- Having a performance development plan (PDP), and receiving a formal appraisal, are both related to significantly higher levels of engagement. These aspects of working life signal to employees that their training needs and their development, and career aspirations are being taken seriously by the organisation; they also indicate that the individual's line manager cares sufficiently about their direct reports to sit down with them and discuss their future.

5. Understanding the Drivers of Engagement

5.1 Engagement correlations

5.1.1 The key driver

The strongest driver of engagement is a sense of **feeling valued and involved**. This makes intuitive sense, given that the components of the 'feeling valued and involved' indicator relate to several aspects already identified as relevant to engagement:

- involvement in decision-making
- the extent to which employees feel able to voice their ideas, and managers listen to these views, and value employees' contributions
- the opportunities employees have to develop their jobs
- the extent to which the organisation is concerned for employees' health and well-being.

5.1.2 What fosters a sense of value?

The key role of the line manager can be clearly seen — not only as a direct link, but also indirectly, in that the line manager is instrumental in such aspects as delivering performance appraisals, smoothing the path to training, communicating and demonstrating equality of opportunity. A positive feeling of feeling valued and involved is linked to positive views about many aspects of working life, notably:

- training, development and career

- immediate management
- performance and appraisal
- communication
- equal opportunities and fair treatment

5.2 IES' engagement model

The model in Figure 5.1 makes use of the first significant finding that was derived from the research and is described in this report. This is the key role of feeling valued and involved as a driver of engagement. The model indicates that a focus on increasing individuals' perceptions of their involvement with, and value to, the organisation will pay dividends in terms of increased engagement levels.

5.3 IES' diagnostic tool

Figure 5.2 shows the main drivers of employee engagement for the NHS case study described in this report. The diagnostic tool uses the fact that feeling valued and involved is the key driver of engagement, but also shows the main component of feeling valued and involved. The identification of these components

Figure 5.1: The engagement model

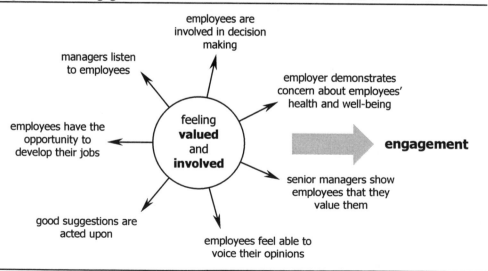

Source: IES, 2003

Figure 5.2: The drivers of employee engagement: a diagnostic tool

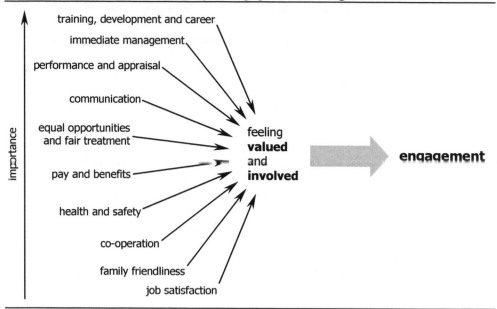

Source: IES, 2003

give a pointer to organisations towards those aspects of working life that require serious attention if engagement levels are to be maintained or improved.

The components of feeling valued and involved, and the relative strength of each driver, are likely to vary depending on the organisation. In addition, different employee groups within one organisation will probably have a slightly different set of drivers.

5.4 Practical implications of the model

There is a clear link between employees' experiences and general perceptions of working life and their sense of being valued and involved — and therefore to their engagement levels, as engagement is closely linked to feeling valued and involved. Engagement is believed to be one step beyond commitment, which has been shown to have an impact on business outcomes; it is also linked to increased intention to stay with the organisation. It therefore makes sense for organisations to monitor the engagement levels of employees, and to take action to increase these.

IES' engagement research indicates that the following areas are of fundamental importance to engagement.

- **Good quality line management** — managers who:
    - care about their employees
    - keep them informed
    - treat them fairly
    - encourage them to perform well
    - take an interest in their career aspirations
    - smooth the path to training and development opportunities.
- **Two-way, open communication** — which allows the employee to voice ideas and suggest better ways of doing things, while at the same time keeping employees informed about the things that are relevant to them (including the relationship between the jobs they have and the wider business).
- **Effective co-operation** within the organisation — between different departments and functions, and also between management and trade unions.
- **A focus on developing employees** — so that individuals feel that the organisation takes a long-term view of their value, and delivers both the training they need now and fair access to development opportunities.
- **A commitment to employee well-being** — demonstrated by taking health and safety seriously, working to minimise accidents, injuries, violence and harassment, and taking effective action should a problem occur.
- **Clear, accessible HR policies and practices** to which line managers and senior managers are committed — particularly with regard to appraisals, equal opportunities and family friendliness.
- **Fairness in relation to pay and benefits** — in terms of comparisons within and outside the organisation.
- **A harmonious working environment** — which encourages employees to respect and help each other.

5.5 The issues and challenges

5.5.1 It works both ways

The two-way nature of engagement has been stressed many times in this report. New recruits often arrive with high engagement levels and a sense of optimism about their future. Organisations cannot expect these levels of engagement to maintain themselves, but instead need to work to nurture the all-important sense of feeling valued and involved.

One thing that engagement has in common with the psychological contract is the ease and rapidity with which it can be shattered; a badly-thought-out, ill-timed or merely clumsy action by the organisation can destroy years of patiently-accumulated goodwill. For this reason, organisations should not embark on an attempt to raise engagement levels unless they are prepared to invest sufficiently into it — time, effort and money. The importance of the line manager in the engagement model, for example, suggests that a major investment in line management development might be needed, while taking health and safety seriously could involve considerable expenditure on new equipment and training.

5.5.2 One size does not (quite) fit all

While the IES model works well as a general approach, employees are not all the same. Organisations using employee attitude surveys to measure engagement levels will be able to compare scores of different groups, and are likely to encounter similar findings to those uncovered in the NHS. That is to say that engagement of different employee groups are not the same. IES' diagnostic tool can be used if the data will support it, to explore whether the drivers of engagement are the same for all groups.

In the NHS, for example, feeling valued and involved is the key driver for employee engagement in every job group except for one — Pharmacists, for whom job satisfaction is the most important factor. There is no clear indication why this should be the case, unless it is something to do with the relative independence of this professional group. Another interesting observation is that the importance of equal opportunities and fair treatment as a driver varies considerably, and in general this variation is linked to the percentage of minority ethnic employees within the job group. For healthcare assistants and nursing auxiliaries (a group with a high percentage of minority ethnic employees) it is the fourth most important contributor to engagement, whereas for community nurses and therapists (with low percentages) it is eleventh and seventh highest respectively.

5.5.3 Professional groups: engagement to what?

The NHS data set revealed an interesting finding with regard to professional groups. Although, in general, employees in these groups have somewhat higher engagement levels than their colleagues in supporting roles, this is by no means the case for all professionals; for example, Doctors and Midwives have lower than average engagement levels, even though their job satisfaction ratings are above average. **It appears that professionals often feel a higher level of commitment and loyalty to their work — and, in the NHS, to their patients — than to their organisation**. This means that professionals may not be very interested in the organisation's aims and values, instead preferring to go wherever they feel they can best practise their craft and receive, in return, the appreciation of their peers and their clients. To some extent, this may not matter to organisations, especially if these individuals perform very effectively while they are employed. However, the fact that the loss of highly skilled people can be a severe blow to organisational performance indicates that it would be worthwhile to try to understand what drives engagement for these key professionals.

5.5.4 The length of service question

The decline in engagement levels as length of service increases represents a big challenge to organisations. Clearly, the knowledge and experience of long-serving employees are of enormous value to the organisation — but their relatively low engagement levels are perhaps blunting the potential impact these individuals could make. All sorts of reasons for lower engagement suggest themselves, such as career frustration (being passed over for promotion), boredom (job has become routine), cynicism (seen it all before) and perhaps disappointment (with themselves or their organisation). Although the effort involved in increasing the engagement levels of long-servers may be considerable, in all but the most hardened of cases, it is probably worthwhile — given the correspondingly greater rewards.

6. Final Words

This report has described IES' research into the concept of employee engagement. This research has resulted in a definition of engagement, has tested engagement statements from which an indicator of engagement has been derived, and has established a model showing the key drivers of engagement.

In addition, the research has analysed the differences in the engagement levels of employee groups, depending on their personal and job characteristics and their experiences at work.

The report draws out, in Chapter 5, the practical implications of the engagement model, together with some engagement issues. These should be of particular value to managers and HR practitioners who want not only to read about this intriguing subject, but also want to take action to improve engagement levels within their organisations. The encouraging news is that it is possible to take action to improve employees' sense of feeling valued and involved, therefore their engagement levels.

Further research by IES is planned, to test the engagement indicator and model in different employment sectors.

Appendix 1: Defining and Creating Employee Commitment: A Review of Current Research

Michael Silverman

Introduction

Over the last ten years, the study of commitment has advanced in many different directions. A variety of disciplines have adopted the topic as a theme in their research and these have offered fresh and significant insights. These recent advances include new approaches to both the conceptualisations of employee commitment and the particular human resource practices intended to increase it.

This review discusses the definition of commitment and its creation based on extensive experience of working in this area and a comprehensive literature review by IES. The bibliography of sources used is given in Appendix 1.

Current research concerning employee commitment highlights the pitfalls of viewing commitment as a one-dimensional construct that can be enhanced by a particular human resource policy. This assumes that a particular practice, for example, offering flexible working arrangements or more training, will have a significant and beneficial effect on employee commitment. Unfortunately, in practice it is not that simple because there is no single solution. All employees' wants and needs cannot be addressed by a single policy.

What is now apparent is that, as long as the organisation has been able to attract the right sort of employees and has provided a suitable work environment, employee commitment will be influenced by the interactions that occur between colleagues and with their immediate and senior managers. Commitment is complex and continuous, and requires employers to discover ways of enhancing the work life of their employees.

The benefits of a committed workforce

The performance benefits accrued from increased employee commitment have been widely demonstrated in the literature. To list but a few, these include:

- increased job satisfaction (Vandenberg and Lance 1992)
- increased job performance (Mathieu and Zajac, 1990)
- increased total return to shareholders (Walker Information Inc., 2000)
- increased sales (Barber *et al.,* 1999)
- decreased employee turnover (Cohen, 1991)
- decreased intention to leave (Balfour and Wechsler, 1996)
- decreased intention to search for alternative employers (Cohen, 1993)
- decreased absenteeism (Cohen, 1993, Barber *et al.,* 1999).

With this in mind, employee commitment should be viewed as a business necessity. Organisations who have difficulty in retaining and replacing competent employees will find it hard to optimise performance. There are not only the immediate expenses of the recruitment process but other hidden costs such as management time and lost productivity as new employees take time to become effective in their roles.

Types of Commitment

In simple terms, we might think of commitment in terms of feelings of obligation or emotional attachment. However, in the last 15 years, a growing consensus has emerged that commitment should be viewed as a multidimensional construct. Allen and Meyer (1990) developed an early model that has received considerable attention. The three-component model they advocated was based on their observation that existing definitions of commitment at that time reflected at least three distinct themes:

1. an affective emotional attachment towards an organisation (affective commitment)

2. the recognition of costs associated with leaving an organisation (continuance commitment), and

3. a moral obligation to remain with an organisation (normative commitment).

One important point is that not all forms of employee commitment are positively associated with superior performance (Meyer and Allen, 1997). For example, an employee who has low affective and normative commitment, but who also has high continuance commitment is unlikely to yield performance benefits. The main reason such an employee remains with an organisation is for the negative reason that the costs associated with leaving are too great.

In more recent years, this typology has been further explored and refined to consider the extent to which the social environment created by the organisation makes employees feel incorporated, and gives them a sense of identity. O'Malley (2000) contends that a review of the commitment literature produces five general factors, which relate to the development of employee commitment:

Affiliative commitment – An organisation's interests and values are compatible with those of the employee, and the employee feels accepted by the social environment of the organisation.

Associative commitment – organisational membership increases employees' self-esteem and status. The employee feels privileged to be associated with the organisation.

Moral commitment – employees perceive the organisation to be on their side and the organisation evokes a sense of mutual obligation in which both the organisation and the employee feel a sense of responsibility to each other. This type of commitment is also frequently referred to in the literature as normative commitment.

Affective commitment – Employees derive satisfaction from their work and their colleagues, and their work environment is supportive of that satisfaction. Some researchers (eg Allen and Meyer, 1990) suggest that this is the most important form of commitment as it has the most potential benefits for organisations. Employees who have high affective commitment are those who will go beyond the call of duty for the good of the organisation. In recent literature this form of commitment has also been referred to as 'engagement' and is the form of commitment that is most usually measured by organisations.

Structural commitment — Employees believe they are involved in a fair economic exchange in which they benefit from the relationship in material ways. There are enticements to enter and remain in the organisation and there are barriers to leave. This type of commitment is also frequently referred to in the literature as continuance commitment.

With reference to the above typology, when an organisation is considering assessing the commitment of its workforce, not only should it ask *how much* commitment exists, but also what *types* of commitment exist.

Antecedents of commitment

Demographics

A range of demographic variables has been found to be related to employee commitment (Mathieu and Zajac, 1990). For a variety of reasons, age has been found to be a positive predictor of employee commitment. As Mathieu and Zajac (1990) suggest, the older employees become, the less employment options are available. As a result, older employees may view their current employment more favourably. In addition, Dunham *et al.* (1994) suggest older employees may be more committed because they have a stronger investment and greater history with their organisation.

With regard to gender, a number of studies (*eg* Mathieu and Zajac, 1990) have reported women as being more committed than men. This is typically explained by women having to overcome more barriers than men to get to their position in the organisation.

Marital status has also been shown to relate to commitment, with married employees usually showing more commitment (Mathieu and Zajac, 1990). However, it is suggested that the reason for this is because married employees will typically have greater financial and family responsibilities, which increases their need to remain with the organisation. Note, however, that this refers to structural commitment (or continuance commitment) in that the cost associated with leaving the organisation increases commitment to the organisation. As mentioned previously, structural commitment does not necessarily relate to increased performance.

Recruitment procedures

O'Malley (2000) suggests that organisations need to pay more attention to addressing employees' social need to affiliate and belong. He argues that employees want to be in an environment that make them feel comfortable. Organisations have goals and values, and people recruited by the organisation should share these. The argument here is that, in order to create commitment, the organisation must have the right sort of employees in the first instance.

Employees' feelings of belonging start to develop long before employees join the organisation. As Parks and Floyd (1996) point out, there are several things organisations can do to make employees feel welcomed and valued as the recruitment and selection process develops. They can:

- share details about the organisation
- provide employees with help and support throughout the recruitment and selection process
- convey the interests and values that the organisation shares with employees.

Organisations need to be attractive to the right sort of people; thus the initial contact between the organisation and the prospective candidate is very important. As Troy (1998) points out, increasingly organisations are attempting to communicate with prospective employees in a coherent manner by developing an *employer brand*. The brand should condense the basic nature of the organisation, what its values are, and what it would be like to work there. The principal purpose of the brand is to efficiently bring employers and employees together, in order to establish a relationship. Thus, a good brand should convey both the unique benefits of the organisational environment, and the type of person who is likely to do well in that setting. The organisation must then ensure that it delivers these promises to its employees, or its efforts will have been wasted.

In relation to this, much of the dialogue between employers and employees who are evaluating one another stays 'safe'. Discussions focus on work and related areas and do not provide an opportunity to explore personal dynamics. Work is done in a social context, and where and with whom it is done is as equally important as the nature of the work itself. Employers should, therefore, devote a portion of the selection process to assessing cultural fit.

Expectations met

This line of research suggests that employees will be more committed if there is a good match between what the person is looking for in a job, and what the job provides (Dawis, 1992). A related notion is that commitment will be greater when employees' experiences on the job match their pre-entry expectations. A meta-analysis by Wanous *et al.* (1992) reported an average correlation of 0.39 between met expectations and commitment. As Sturges and Guest (2000) note, unmet expectations are commonly cited as a cause of dissatisfaction. Such expectations usually relate to the type of work employees are given to do and the opportunities for training and development they receive. With this in mind, realistic job previews (giving candidates real experience of what the job is like) can be very useful. For example, Premack and Wanous (1985) found a high positive correlation between realistic job previews and commitment.

Induction and training

Several studies have demonstrated a link between early job experiences and commitment (*eg* Mignerey *et al.*, 1995). The induction programme should be the final step of the recruitment and selection process. A good induction programme will make new employees more familiar with, and more at ease within, the organisation. Employees enter the organisation with an assumption of compatibility and should be welcomed. This will make new recruits more likely to be receptive to feedback and other interventions that encourage social integration.

Training is also an important part of the induction process. Although commitment is not necessarily the intended, or at least most obvious, objective of training, it can nevertheless be influenced in the process. Gaertner and Nollen (1989) found that commitment was related to employees' perceptions of organisational efforts to provide them with training, but not to their actual training experiences. IES research with numerous organisations also supports the relationship between the provision of training and development opportunities for staff, and increased levels of commitment and job satisfaction.

Relationships with managers

This refers to how the quality of the relationship between managers and their employees relates to the development of commitment. Several studies have found significant positive relationships between the two variables, that is, employees who have good relationships with their immediate managers have greater commitment (Green *et al.*, 1996; Nystrom, 1990; Settoon *et al.*, 1996). Similarly, a recent study by the CIPD (2001) concluded that a good relationship between managers and employees is one of the most important factors affecting motivation at work. Employees' commitment reflects their day to day contacts with their line managers about their job, and the way in which objective targets are set. Effective communication on job-related issues is a key ingredient in securing individual performance.

To a great extent, individual line managers are responsible for ensuring that these maintenance behaviours occur. Indeed, managers are key to creating commitment in an organisation, as was demonstrated in Barber *et al.* (1999). The most well developed organisational programme can break down at the point of transmission with poor management.

Relationships with colleagues

Although emotional attachment to colleagues in the workplace is an important element of commitment, it is not enough on its own. This important aspect, however, must not be neglected but maintained through frequent, pleasurable contact with peers

(Baumeister and Leary, 1995). Unless there is occasion for frequent and rewarding interaction, stronger feelings of belonging that can bind employees to the organisation are unlikely to emerge. Organisations that want to build high levels of commitment should look for ways to build this through group activities both in and out of work.

Group membership

To build commitment, being a member of a particular organisation must not only satisfy employees' social need to affiliate and belong, but must also create a sense of collective identity that differentiates the group from other organisations. There are two ways to achieve this (Hogg *et al.*, 1995):

- establish a social boundary that indicates that an identifiable collection of people or unit exists
- the group must assume some evaluative meaning, *ie* the group has to offer something that the employer wants or needs.

There are many situational features that contribute to a sense of group membership. The more exposure that employees have to these features, the more likely it is that they will feel like a part of the group and incorporate that membership into their concept of who they are.

Organisational justice and trust

It is also argued that employees evaluate their experiences at work in terms of whether they are fair and whether the organisation is concerned for the well-being of the employees (Meyer, 1997). Research findings (*eg* McFarlin and Sweeney, 1992) suggest that employees' commitment to the organisation might be shaped, in part, by their perception of how fairly they are treated by the organisation. The literature supports the idea that organisations communicate their commitment to employees through treating them fairly. Therefore, organisations wanting to foster greater commitment from their employees must first provide evidence of their commitment to employees.

Organisational justice also has links with the concept of trust. According to Kramer (1999), trust in an organisation can promote the acceptance of organisational initiatives. When there is trust, employees are willing to suspend judgement and defer to the authority of others. In addition, trust permits organisational flexibility because a payback need be neither immediate nor of equivalent value. O'Malley (2000) identifies four areas in which employees' sense of trust in the employer can be increased:

- **Growth**: As most employees want to be more proficient in their job, a good way to instil trust is to attend to employees' development needs.
- **Work-life balance**: Most employees would like organisations to allow greater personal time when needed.
- **Individual accommodation**: Acts of organisational flexibility or benevolence toward employees.
- **Health and safety**: Organisations that are committed to protecting employees' health and safety are more likely to be trusted.

Promotion

Policies and practices concerning promotion can also affect commitment. For example, Schwarzwald *et al.* (1992) found that commitment was higher among employees who had been promoted, and was also related to employees' perceptions that the organisation had a preference of recruiting from their internal labour market. Such a policy might be perceived as an example of the organisation's commitment to the employee as discussed earlier. Among those who are considered for promotion, the outcome of the decision is likely to have an effect on commitment. But, for some, the perception of fairness in the decision-making process might be even more important. This suggests that organisations should communicate clearly how their decisions were made and why those who did not succeed were not suitable.

Work-life balance

A key issue emphasised by research, especially in recent years, is the extent to which employee perceive they are able to achieve the right balance between home and work. Organisations are beginning to recognise this, and are making more concerted efforts to introduce a host of programmes intended to ease employees' burdens. These include initiative such as: flexible work arrangements; child care; time off policies; elderly care; health care; information and counselling; and convenience services to name but a few. A major study by the Families and Work Institute (1998) found that such employer support was related to increased employee commitment.

Job satisfaction

How happy an employee is in a job has a profound effect on behaviour and commitment. From meta-analyses (*eg* Iaffaldano and Muchinsky, 1985) it is clear that employees who enjoy their jobs will work harder and stay longer with their employers than employees who do not. In relation to commitment, job satisfaction and work-life satisfaction are very important. Job satisfaction is an enormous area; however, to be concise a satisfying job typically has three properties:

- It has intrinsically enjoyable features — Mathieu and Zajac (1990) found that the strongest correlation with commitment were obtained for job characteristics, particularly job scope (enrichment).
- It provides an opportunity for growth and development.
- It makes employees feel effective in their roles (that they can positively influence organisational outcomes).

A positive relationship between job satisfaction and commitment, using a variety of satisfaction and commitment measures, has been consistently reported in the literature (Balfour and Wechsler, 1990; Cook and Wall, 1980; Green *et al.*, 1996).

Pay and reward

As mentioned previously, employees may remain with an organisation because there are constraints against leaving and incentives for staying. It is important for organisations to structure the economics of the relationship in a way that will not obstruct commitment.

One of the reasons to stay in a relationship is because it makes sense economically. Pay makes continuation of the employment relationship worthwhile because there is mutual dependence. Organisations that add on benefits are establishing the foundation for richer forms of commitment by producing a need for the relationship (*ie* creating dependence).

Empirical tests of the administration of benefits have implications for employee commitment. For example, Grover and Crooker (1995) used data collected in a national survey of over 1,500 US workers to examine the relationship between availability of family-responsive benefits and affective organisational commitment. They found a positive correlation between the availability of such benefits and commitment, even for those who would not benefit directly. They argue that organisations offering such benefits are perceived by employees as showing greater caring and concern, and as being fair in their dealings with employees. Similar research examined the link between organisational commitment and rewards, operationalised as actual income and pay satisfaction. This research found that commitment was more strongly related to pay satisfaction than to actual income.

In summary, as Rusbult and Buunk (1993) contend, people stay in relationships to the extent that they are uniquely dependent on them relative to the alternatives. The more attractive the alternatives and the lower the termination costs, the less people are reliant on their existing relationship for the source of their satisfaction.

Summary and conclusion

This report has presented a review of past and recent thinking about defining and creating employee commitment, which is an evolving topic currently receiving considerable attention. It has been identified as a multi-dimensional concept, which has important impacts on an organisation through its effects on employee performance, turnover and absence, and via its influence on customer attitudes to the bottom line.

Commitment can be divided into five components, each of which are created by different factors. These are defined as follows:

- **Affiliative**: The compatibility of the employee's and the organisation's interests and values.
- **Associative**: The employee's perception of belonging to the organisation.

- **Moral**: The sense of mutual obligation between the employee and the organisation.
- **Affective**: The feeling of job satisfaction experienced by the employee.
- **Structural**: The belief that the employee is engaged in a fair economic exchange.

Affective commitment is the form that has most potential benefit for an organisation, as it directly influences how employees perform their jobs.

Organisations that take positive steps to create commitment appreciate that it is a vital component of business success. They recognise that it can take various forms and are able to concentrate on the ones that are relevant to them. Commitment is a two-way process that the organisation itself has to initiate, by creating a clear employer brand and group identity so that the right people are recruited. The organisation then needs to ensure that the values of its brand image are delivered by treating employees fairly and maintaining trust.

Job satisfaction is an important component of commitment, but should not be perceived as equivalent to it. Commitment has more positive outcomes for the organisation in terms of employee performance. Job satisfaction can be promoted by making work as enjoyable as possible, providing growth and development opportunities and making provisions for staff to assist them in balancing their work and personal lives.

Once established, commitment has to be maintained by ensuring staff have clear roles and responsibilities, and understanding of what is required of them in their jobs. Good communication and openness throughout the organisation is vital, especially in times of change. The role of line managers should be recognised and positively supported, as it is an important component in the creation and maintenance of employee commitment.

Appendix 2: Organisational Citizenship Behaviour: A Review of Current Research

Rob Barkworth

Introduction

Organisational Citizenship Behaviour (OCB) has a research tradition spanning some 20 years, although much of the interest in the concept has only arisen more recently. The purpose of this paper is to explore that research literature so that clear definitions can be presented, to put forward the business case for OCB, discuss antecedents that promote OCB and finally link the research findings to human resource practices.

OCB comprises of a large group of behaviours, ranging from helping colleagues to conveying a positive impression of the organisation to others. Some support has been given to the notion that these behaviours can lead to increased organisational effectiveness, but research of this question is still in its infancy. The vast majority of the research effort has been directed at establishing what causes employees to demonstrate OCB, and from this the practitioner can take ideas to help create an environment whereby performance may be enhanced through OCB.

What is now emerging is that performance gains can be harnessed by consideration of the softer behaviours as well as the harder in-role behaviours, but whereas in-role behaviours may be scrutinised by managers, OCBs are voluntary in nature and harder to discern. An understanding of these issues might lead to competitive advantage.

What is OCB?

Unfortunately there is no simple answer to this question as the research literature has produced a proliferation of definitions and types of OCB. A discussion of these will follow but a good starting point is to consider why interest in the subject started and how OCB was originally conceived. The first ideas of the subject were expressed in an essay by Organ (1977, as cited in Organ and Paine, 1999), where he defended the practitioner idea that satisfaction causes performance. Organ reasoned that although this view had not received empirical support by academics, it was retained by practitioners, maybe because they had a broader view of performance. The traditional view of performance had been in terms of hard outcomes measurable against job descriptions, but what had not been considered were the softer issues such as an employee turning up on time and following organisational rules. OCB was later defined as: *'individual behaviour that is discretionary, not directly or explicitly recognised by the formal reward system, and that in the aggregate promotes the effective running of the organisation.' (Organ, 1988, p.4).*

The first point to note about this definition is that the behaviour is discretionary or extra-role, so that the employee has choice over whether they perform such behaviour. As these types of behaviour are not usually part of the reward system, absence of such behaviours is therefore not punishable by the organisation but performance of them should lead to effective running of it. Before the literature on resultant organisational performance is assessed, it is first necessary to present a typology of behaviours, which fit into the category of OCB.

Typology of OCBs

As has been said previously, many different forms of OCBs have been identified and defined, in fact in their recent review of the subject, Podsakoff *et al.* (2000) detail 30 forms. Their paper classified these behaviours into seven themes:

Helping Behaviour

This involves the voluntarily helping of others, such as assisting those who have fallen behind in their work, and identifying and stopping work-related problems in the first place.

Sportsmanship

Behaviours that come under the banner of sportsmanship include being able to carry on with a positive attitude in the face of adversity, being willing to set aside personal interests for the good of the group and being unfazed by the rejection of suggestions.

Organisational loyalty

This consists of behaviours that involve promoting the organisation to the outside world, and staying committed to it, even when doing so could involve a personal sacrifice.

Organisational compliance

An employee is said to be organisationally compliant when they follow organisational rules even when not being monitored. This is considered an OCB even though the rules are considered 'in-role', as it is the case that many employees simply do not follow all of the rules all of the time.

Individual initiative

This set of behaviours is considered to be OCB, as it demonstrates performance over and above what is expected. Behaviours include working with extreme enthusiasm, taking on extra roles and showing an interest in improving the way things are done in order to increase performance.

Civic virtue

This is demonstrated by behaviours that show a macro-level interest in the organisation as a whole, such as a loyal citizen would display towards their country. Examples of such behaviours include volunteering and taking an interest in organisational committees and being vigilant for threats to the organisation.

Self-development

These behaviours include voluntarily improving one's own knowledge, skills and abilities in such a way as to be helpful to the organisation. This form of OCB requires a longer-term focus than the others and implies a commitment to the organisation extending well into the future.

As this typology demonstrates, there are many varieties of behaviour that come under the banner of OCB. Also, as will be discussed later, different antecedents are responsible for promoting different types of OCB. With this in mind, another useful classification of OCB, which has been advocated by several researchers (Barbuto *et al.*, 2003; Turnley *et al.*, 2003) is that of citizenship behaviours either directed at the organisation (OCB-O) or at the individual (OCB-I). Having defined the various types of OCB, its impact on organisational effectiveness will now be considered.

Consequences of OCB

The final part of Organ's (1988) definition of OCB was that it promotes effective running of the organisation. Surprisingly little work has been produced to test this proposition empirically; the bulk of the studies examine the link between job satisfaction and OCB. Although Organ's statement makes intuitive sense, without empirical analysis there seems little point gearing human resource policies to promote an outcome that might not be beneficial. In fact Podsakoff *et al.* (2000) report that of the 160 papers on the topic, only five had tested the organisational effectiveness link.

Organisational level outcomes

The first to test this proposition (Karambayya, 1990, as cited in Podsakoff *et al.*, 2000) found that employees in high-performing work units were more likely to exhibit OCB than those in low-performing units. However, this study relied on subjective reporting of unit performance, made by different individuals in the 12 participating organisations, so doubts are raised about the reliability of results produced. Unfortunately, this paper could not be retrieved, as it was unpublished, but of the authors who cite it none made any reference to the type of OCB being measured.

More recent research has found that although some forms of OCB result in organisational effectiveness, others seem to hinder it (Podsakoff and MacKenzie, 1994). This study occurred in a large insurance organisation, which had a high turnover of staff. They found that sportsmanship and civic virtue correlated positively with departmental success but helping behaviours did not. They put forward several reasons why this may be the case. First, whilst the recipient of the helping behaviour might benefit and therefore increase performance, this might limit the help provider's output due to the time spent helping. One would assume that this would eventually increase performance overall, as the new recruit learnt the job, but the authors reason that, due to high turnover, the resultant gains might never be realised. Another reason why helping behaviours did not, in this instance, produce performance gains is that the assistance provided was, in fact, not necessarily helpful to the recipient. So the results of this study, whilst providing some evidence in support of OCB increasing organisational effectiveness, do raise the issue that the context in which OCB occurs needs to be taken into consideration. This suggests that OCB might not be suitable in all circumstances.

More substantial support for the OCB/performance link comes from a study based in a paper mill, where both quantity and quality of performance was measured (Podsakoff *et al.*, 1997). Encouragingly, the results showed that both sportsmanship and helping behaviour had a significant impact on quantity, while helping behaviour impacted on performance quality. They explain this performance gain in terms of workers helping each other out, by expertise sharing and trying to prevent problems in the future. There are comparisons between this stream of work and that of job design. In particular, a study by Wall *et al.*, (1992) showed that when machine operators were given more autonomy to rectify faults, downtime of the machines decreased and, so as a result, . Relating this back to the Podsakoff *et al.* (1997) study, it could be said that helping behaviour only assisted in this instance because workers were given autonomy, so that they could use their knowledge to prevent future problems. This again highlights the importance of the context in which OCB occurs, and their interaction with other policies and practices already in place.

More evidence comes from Walz and Niehoff (1994, as cited in Podsakoff *et al.*, 2000) who found that employees in high-performing fast-food restaurants demonstrated more OCB than those in low-performing restaurants. In terms of specific behaviours, helping behaviour was associated with greater operating efficiency, customer satisfaction and income generated per member of staff, and was negatively linked to waste. Also, civic virtue and sportsmanship were negatively related to complaints from customers.

Finally, more research conducted in the insurance sales sector revealed that employees who display higher levels of OCB are perceived by customers to provide better service quality (Bell and Menguc, 2002). The authors' reason that this is due both to customer-oriented OCB, and OCB that increases internal organisational effectiveness.

In the review by Podsakoff *et al.* (2000) they conclude that studies so far have supported the idea of the link between OCB and organisational performance, although the link is greater for some kinds of OCB (such as helping behaviour) than others (such as sportsmanship and civic virtue). The findings do tend to suggest that improvements can be made when employees demonstrate OCB, so it would therefore be a fruitful line of inquiry to discover how to promote such behaviours in the first place.

Individual outcomes

Besides organisational-level outcomes, efforts have been put into seeing what the consequences are for those who demonstrate OCB. A study (MacKenzie *et al.*, 1991) examined the evaluations or appraisals managers make of their employees, and found that OCB (in the form of altruism and civic virtue) counts as much, in the formation of evaluations, as objective performance levels. This finding raises the concern that employees are being appraised not only against their job descriptions but also against unwritten criteria, which could be deemed unfair. OCB, by its definition, is extra-role and voluntary — so employees who are performing all their job tasks maximally, but are unaware that they are also being assessed on OCB, could become de-motivated by a poor appraisal outcome. This problem could be overcome by incorporating OCB into the organisation's values and ethos, which would signal that these are desired behaviours.

Another individual outcome of interest is that of the relationship between demonstrating OCB and turnover. Chen *et al.*, (1998) found that employees who exhibited lower levels of OCB were more likely to leave the organisation. There was a longitudinal element to this study, and so not only was there a negative correlation between OCB and intentions to quit, but also in actual turnover. This finding adds a further dimension to the use of the study of OCB, as it not only has implications in terms of performance, but also impacts on retention.

Antecedents of OCB

Given that the research suggests that a workforce that is demonstrating OCB results in increased organisational effectiveness, what causes OCB in the first place and what human resource policies can be implemented to promote it?

Attitudinal predictors

Attitudinal predictors, such as job satisfaction, organisational commitment, leader supportiveness and fairness correlate with OCB at similar levels (0.23-0.31) which suggests that there might be an overall 'morale' factor which accounts for OCB (Organ and Ryan, 1995). Recent research examined the fairness predictor further (Williams et al., 2002), and revealed that the most important aspect of fairness was that of fair treatment by supervisors. As this perception increased in the individual, so did the likelihood of demonstrating OCB. Interestingly, perceptions of fair rewards and fair formal procedures were not predictors of OCB intentions.

OCB and the psychological contract

Linked to the issue of fairness is the stream of work examining the psychological contract and OCB. Psychological contracts refer to the (usually unwritten) beliefs individuals have, regarding promises made between themselves and their employer (Rousseau, 1995). When this contract is broken by the employer it has been found that this can have knock-on effects on an employee's job satisfaction, organisational commitment and OCB. Turnley et al. (2003) found that although psychological contract breach is related to in-role performance and to OCB directed towards both the organisation and the individual, the strongest link is to OCB directed towards the organisation. That is, they are most likely to withdraw OCB that is organisationally centred when an employee perceives the psychological contract to have been broken by their employer. Breaking these results down further, it was found that breach concerning the employment relationship was more significant than that of pay. There was also evidence to suggest that when reasons as to why a contract has been breached are adequately communicated by the organisation, the resultant dip in performance (both in- and extra-role) will be lessened. This is in agreement with previous research (Robinson, 1996), who also found that the dip in performance is less likely to occur in organisations where levels of trust were at a high level before breach.

OCBs and abusive supervision

Again linked to the idea of fairness is the concept of 'abusive supervision', which includes behaviour that is bullying, tyrannical, and undermining (Zellars *et al.*, 2002). Not surprisingly, it has been found, in a military environment in America, that those who have abusive supervision demonstrate less OCB than others. The authors also found that this effect was greater for those who themselves defined OCB as extra-role, as they perceived that they did not have to demonstrate such behaviours. However, rare abusive supervision is, it is important for organisations to take the issue seriously, not only out of moral obligation but also because it could also impact on the 'bottom line'.

Dispositional predictors

Organ and Ryan's (1995) meta-analysis also reviewed the theory that dispositional variables are predictors of OCB. They reasoned that an individual's dispositions, such as agreeableness, affectivity and conscientiousness, predispose people to certain states whereby they are more likely to receive treatment that is satisfying, fair and rewarding. So it is argued that a person's dispositions can influence the OCB they demonstrate, by having an effect on their general morale. The results for this line of work are somewhat disappointing. Significant correlations have been found between dispositions and various forms of OCB. However, when Organ, Ryan (1995), in their review of such studies, excluded those relying on self-report of OCB (amid concerns that this produced artificially high levels) most of the correlations became non-significant, with the exception of the correlation between conscientiousness and generalised compliance.

Demographic predictors

The meta-analysis conducted by Podsakoff *et al.* (2000) includes four studies, which examine the link between job tenure and OCB, and five that examine gender. Both these demographics fail to produce significant correlations with demonstration of OCB. They found the finding surprising that gender was not related to OCB, considering that sound theoretical arguments had been put forward that certain types of OCB were more female-typed (altruism) or male-typed (civic virtue). Later research (Kidder, 2002) examined this idea further and found that those in a predominantly female-gender occupation (nursing) were more likely to demonstrate female-typed altruism than those in male-gendered occupations (engineering), who were more likely to demonstrate male-typed civic virtue behaviours. They also found a similar pattern for those who had a more feminine than masculine identity. This does present an issue for organisations, as demonstration of certain types of OCB might be related by gender and so, by extension, performance ratings might also be influenced by gender.

Task-related predictors

Three types of task characteristic — feedback, routinisation, and intrinsically satisfying tasks — have been linked to OCB in a variety of studies. In their meta-analysis, Podsakoff *et al.* (2000) found that they were all significantly correlated with altruism, courtesy, conscientiousness, sportsmanship, and civic virtue. The relationships were in the positive direction, apart from task routinisation, which was linked to the demonstration of fewer types of OCB.

Another type of task, that of being involved in decision-making, was investigated and was found to have a positive effect on the demonstration of OCB (VanYpren *et al.*, 1999). The authors found that the more employees take part in decision-making, the more OCB they demonstrate (altruism, conscientiousness, sportsmanship, courtesy and civic virtue). The results also suggest that it was not partaking in the decision-making itself, but the perceived management support as a result, that led to the demonstration of OCB.

Organisational predictors

Podsakoff *et al.* (2000) found that the only organisational level predictor with any consistency in relation to OCB was group cohesiveness, which correlates positively with OCB.

Leadership-style predictors

Various styles of leadership style have been identified and tested to see the effect they have on subordinates' level of OCB. Reviewing these leadership-style predictors, Podsakoff *et al.*, (2000) indicated that transformational leadership (leadership that involves a charismatic element, inspirational motivation, intellectual stimulation, and individualised consideration) correlated significantly with altruism, courtesy, conscientiousness, and sportsmanship. Two types of transactional leadership (which consists of contingent or non-contingent reward or punishment) correlated with OCB. Contingent reward had a positive relationship, while non-contingent punishment had a negative relationship. Supportive leadership and leader role clarification (aspects of the Path-Goal theory of leadership) were found to correlate with altruism, courtesy, conscientiousness and sportsmanship, the former correlating with civic virtue as well.

Antecedents overview

The review of antecedents presents clear evidence that leadership style has clear effects on the OCB exhibited by employees. This is unsurprising given that leaders have a big impact on their subordinates and that other antecedents that have been identified, such as breach of the psychological contract or abusive supervision. Even if leaders do not have control over all decisions that affect their employees, they can still have an impact on how these decisions are communicated and implemented.

Summary and conclusions

This paper has reviewed the current literature on OCB, to present clear definitions, examine the organisational benefits and discuss likely methods of encouraging such behaviours.

OCB has been classified into seven distinct themes: helping behaviour, sportsmanship, organisational loyalty, organisational compliance, individual initiative, civic virtue, and self-development.

In terms of organisational effectiveness, there are few studies; however, helping behaviour, sportsmanship and civic virtue (which seem to be the most researched areas) appear to lead to performance gains.

The fact that helping behaviour was not beneficial in all studies (Podsakoff and MacKenzie, 1994) raises the issue of context in which the behaviours are to occur, as they will not be suitable in all situations.

Two individual level outcomes of importance to organisations were identified. Demonstration of OCB does seem to count in the appraisal arena, although OCB is extra-role. Also, demonstration of OCB is predictive of turnover, so the concept can also be used in the retention arena.

Having established that OCB has an advantageous effect on the organisation, factors that promote them were then discussed. Attitudinal variables such as job satisfaction, organisational commitment, fairness and leader supportiveness all have a positive relationship with OCB which, it is hypothesised, might be caused by some underlying morale factor.

Other factors, which have been found to be antecedents of OCB, include breach of the psychological contract, abusive supervision, and task-related variables. All of these issues are, in some way, linked to leadership style and behaviour, either directly or more subtly. For the practitioner, the obvious starting place in trying to harness OCB should then be from the top-down, as the impact made by leaders and managers does seem to affect the demonstration of OCB.

Appendix 3: Royal Bank of Scotland Case Study

Helen Wolfe

Background

The Royal Bank of Scotland Group (RBS) is one of Europe's leading financial services groups. By market capitalisation it is the second largest bank in the UK and in Europe and ranks fifth in the world. The Group incorporates a wide-range of brands, including Nat West, Ulster Bank, Tesco Personal finance and Direct Line Insurance.

In 2003, the RBS reported staff costs of £4.3bn, up from £3.94bn in 2002 (RBS Published Accounts, 2002). Clearly, human capital is a key focus in achieving the group goals of generating superior sustainable value for shareholders, by adding value for customers and employees. Evoking and maintaining employee engagement became a key objective of group HR, who looked to investigate the nature of engagement within RBS, and ways in which it varied for different segments of their employee population.

Objectives

A wealth of HR data was available to RBS, and making appropriate use of such information was a primary objective of the HR team. The view was that once an accurate measure of employee engagement could be made and managed effectively, a demonstrable link could be established between levels of this engagement and achieving the primary business objectives. RBS assessed engagement levels in two distinct ways:

- by staff segmentation, including:
  - tenure
  - seniority
  - location
  - gender
- by linking with business objectives and HR data, including;
  - staff turnover
  - productivity
  - absence
  - reward profile.

By examining the precursors, influences, and consequences of engagement in this way, RBS sought to identify the main drivers of engagement in relation to key business issues, such as turnover and productivity. Attention could then shift to identifying the opportunities and threats to engagement, and prioritising business activities to enhance and maintain engagement levels, and ultimately achieve improved and sustained returns to shareholders.

Methodology

A large amount of HR related data was available within RBS, from a variety of sources including:

- employee attitude and opinion surveys
- pulse surveys
- HR Management Systems Data
- joiner survey
- leaver surveys.

The complementary nature of these data sources, enabled the results from over 7,000 employees to be combined and mapped against an eight-factor model of employee engagement. The primary objectives of this were to assess how, and why employees were, or were not engaged, and then investigate this further in relation to organisational data, for example, staff turnover and bank productivity figures. In doing so, this would help to develop an organisation specific model of how

Figure A3.1: Three-point model of engagement

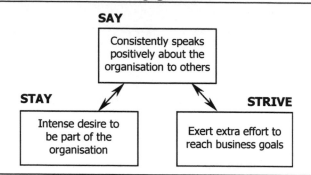

Source: Hewitt, Bacon and Woodrow/Royal Bank of Scotland, 2003

engagement varies within RBS, and how engagement as a tested concept could be used to assess the effectiveness of various strategies (reward, promotion routes, work-life balance *etc.*).

One such example, is the work of Hewitt, Bacon and Woodrow (Hewitt Associates) who define engagement in their three-point model: **'Say', 'Stay', 'Strive'** (Figure A3.1).

RBS adopted this definition of employee engagement, with eight 'drivers' below this (see Table A3.1), which impact on engagement to different degrees. Below each driver is a selection of questions, which can be used to better understand how engagement is influenced.

RBS findings

By combining and analysing data from a range of cross organisational sources, RBS were able to map levels of employee engagement as defined by these sources, and differentiate the involvement of employee engagement on key staff segmentations, and primary business objectives.

Figure A3.2 below shows *example* data, not for RBS as a whole, and indicates the level of agreement for each category.

Table A3.1: RBS employee engagement model: eight 'drivers' of engagement

Factor	Description	Influenced by
Leadership	*'The way the organisation's leaders are perceived by key internal and external stakeholders'*	Leadership Quality of senior team Job security
Product brands and reputation	*'The image and reputation of RBS and its brands, based on perceptions of the group as a corporate citizen and the value and quality of it's service'*	Quality and performance Image and prestige Role in the community
Work itself	*'Sense of accomplishment derived from work'*	Interest Autonomy Systems/Process Tools and resources
Relationships	*'The quality of interrelations with immediate manager, colleagues and customers.'*	Manager Colleagues Clients/Customer
Total reward	*'Total package that the individual receives in return for their contribution to the workplace.'*	Salary element Variable pay Retirement benefits Sharing in success
Recognition	*'Non-financial reward and acknowledgement that the individual receives in return for their contribution in the workplace.'*	Informal recognition Informal manager feedback Formal, non-financial recognition programmes
Performance and development	*'Support to optimise individual/team contribution and opportunities to learn and grow.'*	Job related skill development Career development Internal mobility Performance management
Work-life balance and physical environment	*'The balance between work and personal commitments and the appropriateness of the workplace.'*	Working hours Ways of working Location Workstation design

Source: Royal Bank of Scotland, 2003

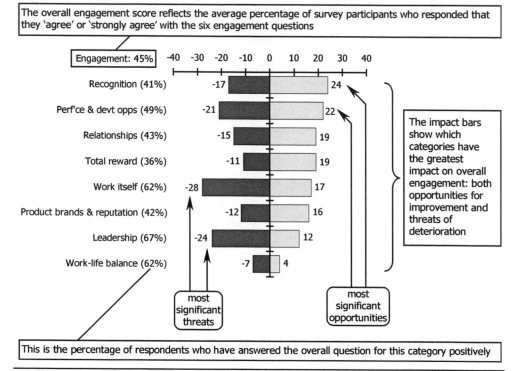

Source: *Royal Bank of Scotland*

Staff segmentation

The levels of staff engagement were also examined by tenure and position within RBS, and in each area the key opportunities and threats to developing and maintaining strong employee

Table A3.2: RBS employee engagement by tenure (per cent)

Length of tenure	Average level of employee engagement
<1 year	50
1-3 years	44
3-5 years	34
5-10 years	39
10+ years	48

Source: *Royal Bank of Scotland, 2003*

Figure A3.3: Engagement and turnover (example data)

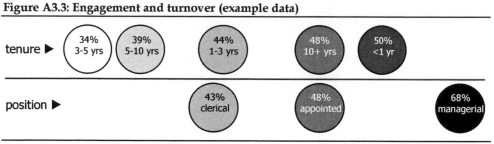

tenure ▶

34% 3-5 yrs 　 39% 5-10 yrs 　 44% 1-3 yrs 　 48% 10+ yrs 　 50% <1 yr

position ▶

43% clerical 　 48% appointed 　 68% managerial

Source: Royal Bank of Scotland

engagement were identified. The relationship between levels of engagement and staff turnover was also explored in a trial area, and over a four month period, a correlation co-efficient −0.43 was found, (this change in turnover would require a (2.7/0.43) 6.3 per cent increase in engagement. Not sure I'd like to go into specifics of changes.) This could be altered to say the correlation was −0.43, which indicates that a two per cent increase in engagement would lead to a 0.86 per cent decrease in staff turnover.

Again, this segmentation below is using example data, and does not represent RBS as a whole.

Employee engagement — differences by tenure

The relationship between tenure and the various facets of engagements within RBS was clearly complex, with different factors providing opportunities and threats to this engagement for different groups of staff. Overall engagement was strongest within the first year of service, and typically declined from one to five years' tenure, increasing slightly from five to ten years and again after ten years' service was reached. Despite this increase, levels of engagement did not reach the high point experienced by those in their first year of joining RBS, where 50 per cent of the staff were positively engaged with the organisation and their work.

By examining the differences in engagement between levels of employees, it was found that engagement was considerably higher for managerial (68 per cent engaged) than clerical (43 per cent engaged). However, staff at appointed level had a significantly lower level of engagement (48 per cent) than their managerial colleagues, and only slightly higher engagement level than that of clerical workers. Again, the drivers of this engagement differed between employment grade, with appointed employees being strongly impacted by the effects of business leadership, whereas the engagement of both managerial and clerical staff was most significantly affected by issues relating to learning and development. By analysing the data across these staff segmentations, RBS were able to identify key opportunities for increasing and maintaining high levels of employee engagement. Both recognition, and learning and development were seen as imperative to all three groups of staff, and in addition the most influential dimensions were highlighted for each staff group:

Factors affecting employee engagement by seniority

- Managerial
  - Work-life balance
- Appointed
  - Total rewards
- Clerical
  - Product brands (quality products)
  - Relationships (customers).

By identifying these key areas of opportunity, RBS are able to focus efforts in a strategic and targeted way, in order to positively affect employee engagement levels, and ultimately assist in fulfilling the primary business objectives.

Subsequent to the initial studies, there has been much work on embedding the engagement model in parts of the RBS group. Following the group-wide employee opinion survey in January 2003, further links between engagement and business measures have been found. In parts of RBS's 'manufacturing' division (centralised processing centres), there was found to be a correlation of 0.30 between engagement and productivity. Therefore a one per cent increase in engagement in those areas would lead to a 0.3 per cent increase in productivity.

Within RBS's Retail Banking division, all HR initiatives are now aligned to the eight engagement 'drivers'. Therefore the division can prioritise which initiatives will have the greatest impact on the engagement of their employees.

What will be done to improve engagement in the organisation? Following work to understand engagement in RBS's Retail Direct division (Tesco Personal Finance, the One Account, credit cards, *etc.*), focus groups were set up to understand the 'recognition' driver in more detail, and how it could be improved.

Appendix 4: Employee Engagement and Related Indicators

This appendix gives details of all the indicators used in the NHS case study questionnaire, that were found to have a relationship with engagement. The majority of these indicators were made up of attitude statements, given below in italics.

Unless indicated, all statements are scored on a five-point scale ranging from one (strongly disagree) to five (strongly agree). Where a statement is negatively worded, the scoring has been reversed, to enable high scores to indicate positive views throughout. These statements are asterisked.

Engagement indicator

I speak highly of this Trust to my friends

I would be happy for my friends and family to be treated here

This Trust is known as a good employer

This Trust has a good reputation generally

I am proud to tell others I am part of this Trust

This Trust really inspires the very best in me in the way of job performance

I find that my values and the Trust's are very similar

I always do more than is actually required

I try to help others in this Trust whenever I can

I try to keep abreast of current developments in my area

I volunteer to do things outside my job that contribute to the Trust's objectives

I frequently make suggestions to improve the work of my team/department/service

Related indicators

Feeling valued and involved

I feel involved in decisions that affect my work
Managers are keen to get staff views on key decisions
I get the opportunity to develop new and better ways of doing my job
I feel valued by senior management
Good suggestions from staff tend to get ignored here*
I feel able to voice my ideas and opinions
The Trust is concerned about my health and well-being

Co-operation

Unions and management work well together to solve problems
Co-operation between departments is good in this Trust
The Joint Staff Committee is an effective forum for communication

Training, development and career

I am encouraged to develop new skills
My line manager takes staff development seriously
I am able to get time off work for training
I have many opportunities for training
I am given adequate training to do my current job
My training needs are regularly discussed
I feel I have equal access to training and development opportunities
This Trust actively supports my continuing professional development

Communication

People are kept informed when changes occur in this Trust
The information I need to do my job is readily available
The grapevine is the most efficient communication channel around here*

Equal opportunities and fair treatment

I feel I am fairly treated here

My work environment is free from bullying and harassment

To be accepted here your face has to fit*

I feel I have a fair chance to apply for internal vacancies

This Trust makes its positive commitment to equal opportunities clear

This Trust provides a service to patients that is free from discrimination

Family friendliness

This Trust is a 'family-friendly' employer

People in this organisation with family commitments have equal career opportunities

This Trust provides good support for staff with family responsibilities

Part-timers have equal access to career progression

Health and safety

Satisfaction is measured, on a five-point scale ranging from one (very dissatisfied) to five (very satisfied), with the following aspects:

Your physical working environment

Health and safety training in this Trust

The cleanliness of the working environment

Your access to staff counselling

Your manager's attitude to health and safety issues

The quality of equipment you use in your job

Your access to Occupational Health Services (excluding counselling)

Security in your workplace

Job satisfaction

There is a lot of variety in my job

I do interesting and challenging work

I get a feeling of accomplishment from my job

Immediate management

My immediate manager is sensitive to work/life issues
My immediate manager lets me know how I am doing
I have a good working relationship with my immediate manager
My immediate manager supports me when things go wrong

Pay and benefits

Good performance is rewarded fairly here
I am rewarded fairly in view of my experience

Performance and appraisal

I am given regular feedback on my performance by my manager
My immediate manager takes performance appraisal seriously

Racial discrimination policy

This Trust has taken effective actions in preventing all forms of racial harassment

I am confident that effective action will be taken to tackle racial harassment when it occurs

The work environment is free from ethnic discrimination

Sex discrimination policy

My work environment is free from sexual harassment
This Trust is slow to deal with cases of discrimination*
Men and women have the same chance of doing well in the Trust

Colleagues

I am treated with respect by the staff I work with
I do not feel part of an efficient team*
I have a good working relationship with my work colleagues

Current career intentions

Respondents were asked to select one of the following:

1. Plan to leave as soon as possible
2. Likely to leave within the next year
3. Likely to stay for at least another year
4. Plan to stay for the foreseeable future

Disability policy

This Trust is good at supporting disabled employees
Facilities for disabled employees are good in this Trust

Burnout

*I feel emotionally drained by my work**
*I feel burned out by my work**

Likely stayers and leavers

As for current career intentions, but collapsed into a two-point scale so that one and two represent 'likely leavers' and three and four 'planned stayers'.

Stress and work pressure

*I feel I am under too much work pressure**
*The demands of the job seriously interfere with my private life**
*I have felt under constant strain recently**
*I have been losing sleep over my work problems**

Reaction to change

*I sometimes feel overwhelmed by the pace of change here**
*The pace of change is too fast here**

Appendix 5: Engagement Statistics

Engagement relationships

Engagement links

The engagement indicator has clear links to other aspects of working life. Positive attitudes about engagement are linked to positive attitudes towards many other aspects of working life. In particular, high engagement levels are associated with positive views about:

- feeling valued and involved
- co-operation in the organisation
- communication
- training, development and career
- equal opportunities and fair treatment.

Each of these aspects is, like the engagement indicator, made up of several attitude statements. Appendix 4 gives the details of these statements. The statistically minded reader can find more information in this appendix. Table A5.1 relates engagement to a variety of other attitudes and experiences expressed by respondents to the NHS survey used to test the engagement variable. All the correlations are highly significant — that is, there is a greater than 99 per cent probability that the association really exists, and is *not* due to chance. All except one are positive, which means that an increase is associated with a higher engagement level — so, for example, higher levels of satisfaction with communication are associated with higher engagement scores. The exception is length of service, which is negatively correlated — that is, engagement levels go down as length of service increases.

Table A5.1: Highly significant engagement relationships

Attitude/experience	Correlation coefficient	N
Feeling valued and involved	0.588	9,941
Co-operation	0.515	9,868
Communication	0.481	9,933
Training, development and career	0.485	9,943
Equal opportunities and fair treatment	0.479	9,911
How the Trust compares as a place to work with two years ago*	0.452	7,267
Job satisfaction	0.410	9,944
Immediate management	0.401	9,941
Pay and benefits	0.398	9,904
Performance and appraisal	0.381	9,923
Colleagues	0.280	9,934
Current career intentions	0.257	9,700
Stress and work pressure	0.155	9,930
Number of days spent on formal training and development in the last 12 months	0.069	9,459
Length of service	−0.062	9,744

Note: Not including employees with less than two years' service

Source: IES, 2003

Regression

Using a statistical regression model shows the extent to which feeling valued and involved is the key driver of engagement. On its own, feeling valued and involved accounts for over 34 per cent of the variation in engagement scores, indicating that feeling valued and involved is a very powerful predictor of engagement. The following six variables account for over 47 per cent of the variation, which is unusually high for a regression model: feeling valued and involved, co-operation, job satisfaction, equal opportunities and fair treatment, ethnicity (white/minority ethnic) and communication.

Feeling valued and involved: correlations

Table A5.2 gives the components of feeling valued and involved, showing only those associations that are highly significant.

Again, almost all the correlations are positive. The two negative correlations are age and length of service — meaning that the sense of feeling valued and involved diminishes as both age and length of service increase.

Table A5.2: Highly significant associations with feeling valued and involved

Attitude/experience	Correlation coefficient	N
Training, development and career	0.689	9,940
Immediate management	0.636	9,940
Performance and appraisal	0.616	9,938
Communication	0.614	9,950
Equal opportunities and fair treatment	0.592	9,915
Pay and benefits	0.532	9,919
How the Trust compares as a place to work with two years ago*	0.478	7,274
Co-operation	0.473	9,866
Job satisfaction	0.409	9,937
Colleagues	0.355	9,934
Current career intentions	0.302	9,703
Stress and work pressure	0.273	9,929
Length of service	−0.090	9,755
Age	−0.076	9,644
Number of days spent on formal training and development in the last 12 months	0.066	9,459

Note: Not including employees with less than two years' service

Source: IES, 2003

Bibliography

Allen N, Meyer J (1990), 'The measurement and antecedents of affective, continuance, and normative commitment to the organisation', *Journal of Occupational Psychology*, Vol. 63, pp. 1-18

Balfour D, Wechsler B (1990), 'Organizational commitment: A reconceptionalization and empirical test of public-private differences, *Review of Public Personnel Administration*, Vol. 10(3), pp. 23-40

Balfour D, Wechsler B (1996), 'Organizational commitment: Antecedents and outcomes in public organisations', *Public Productivity and Management Review*, Vol. 29, pp. 256-277

Barber L, Hayday S, Bevan S (1999), *From people to profits*, IES Report 355

Barbuto J E, Brown L L, Wheeler D W, Wilhite M S (2003), 'Motivation, altruism, and generalized compliance: A field study of organizational citizenship behaviors', *Psychological Reports*, Vol. 92, pp. 498-502

Bauer T, Maertz C, Dolen M, Campion M (1998), 'The Longitudinal assessment of applicant reactions to employment testing and test outcome feedback', *Journal of Applied Psychology*, Vol. 83, pp. 892-903

Baumeister R, Leary M (1995), 'The need to belong: Desire for interpersonal attachments as a fundamental human motivation', *Psychological Bulletin*, Vol. 117, pp. 497-529

Bell S J, Menguc B (2002), 'The employee-organisation relationship, organizational citizenship behaviors, and superior service quality', *Journal of Retailing*, Vol. 78, pp. 131-146

Chen X P, Hui C, Sego D J (1998), 'The role of organizational citizenship behavior in turnover: Conceptualisation and preliminary tests of key hypotheses', *Journal of Applied Psychology*, Vol. 81(3), pp. 922-931

CIPD (2001), *Employers' perceptions of the psychological contract'*, CIPD Report 112

Cohen A (1991), 'Career stage as a moderator of the relationship between organisational commitment and its outcomes: A meta-analysis', *Journal of Occupational Psychology*, Vol. 64, pp. 253-268

Cohen A (1992), 'Antecedents of organisational commitment across occupational groups: A Meta-Analysis', *Journal of Organisational Behaviour*, Vol. 13, pp. 539-558

Cohen A (1993), 'Age and tenure in relation to organisational commitment: A meta-analysis', *Basic and Applied Social Psychology*, Vol. 14, pp. 143-159

Cook J, Wall T (1980), 'New work attitude measures of trust, organisational commitment and personal need non-fulfilment', *Journal of Occupational Psychology*, Vol. 53, pp. 39-52

Dawis R (1992), 'Person-environment fit and job satisfaction', In Cranny C J, *et al.* (eds), *Job Satisfaction*, New York: Lexington

Dindia K, Canary D (1993), 'Definitions and theoretical perspectives on maintaining relationships', *Journal of Social and Personal Relationships*, Vol. 10, pp. 163-173

Dunham R, Grube J, Castaneda M (1994), 'Organisational Commitment: The utility of an integrative definition', *Journal of Applied Psychology*, Vol. 79, pp. 370-380

Gaertner K, Nollen S (1989), 'Career experiences, perceptions of employment practices, and psychological commitment to the organisation', *Human Relations*, Vol. 42, pp. 975-991

Green S, Anderson S, Shivers S (1996), 'Demographics and organisational influences on leader-member exchange and related work attitudes', *Organisational Behaviour and Human Decision Processes*, Vol. 66, pp. 203-214

Grover S, Crooker K (1995), 'Who appreciates family-responsive human resource policies: The impact of family-friendly policies on organisational attachment', *Personnel Psychology*, Vol. 48, pp. 271-288

Harter J K, Schmidt F L, Hayes T L (2002), 'Business-Unit-Level Realtionship Between Employee Satisfaction, Employee Engagement, and Business Outcomes: A Meta-Analysis' *Journal of Applied Psychology*, Vol. 87, No. 2, pp. 268-279

Hogg M, Terry D, White K (1995), 'A tale of two theories: A critical comparison of identity theory with social identity theory', *Social Psychology Quarterly*, Vol. 58, pp. 255-269

Iaffaldano M, Muchinsky P (1985), 'Job satisfaction and job performance: A meta analysis', *Psychological Bulletin*, Vol. 97, pp. 251-273

Kahn W A (1990), 'Psychological Conditions of Personal Engagement and Disengagement at Work' *Academy of Management Journal*, Vol. 33, No. 4, pp. 692-724

Karambayya R (1999), *Contexts for organizational citizenship behavior: Do high performing and satisfying units have better 'citizens'?* York University working paper

Kidder D L (2002), 'The influence of gender on the performance of organizational citizenship behaviors', *Journal of Management*, Vol. 28(5), pp. 629-648

Kramer R (1999), 'Trust and distrust in organisations: Emerging perspectives, enduring questions', *Annual Review of Psychology*, Vol. 50, pp. 569-598

MacKenzie S B, Podsakoff P M, Fetter R (1991), 'Organizational citizenship behaviour and objective productivity as determinants of managerial evaluations of Salespersons' performance', *Organizational Behavior and Human Decision Processes*, Vol. 50, pp. 123-150

Mathieu J, Zajac D (1990), 'A review and meta-analysis of the antecedents, correlates, and consequences of organisational commitment', *Psychological Bulletin*, Vol. 108, pp. 171-194

McFarlin D, Sweeney P (1992), 'Distributive and procedural justice as predictors of satisfaction with personal and organisational outcomes', *Academy of Management Journal*, Vol. 35, pp. 626-637

Meyer J (1997), 'Organisational commitment', in Cooper C I, Robertson I T (eds), *International Review of Industrial and Organisational Psychology*, Vol. 12, pp. 175-228

Mignerey J, Rubin R, Gordon W (1995), 'Organisational entry: An investigation of newcomer communication behaviour and uncertainty', *Communication Research*, Vol. 22, pp. 54-85

Nystrom P (1990), 'Vertical exchanges and organisational commitments of American business managers,' *Group and Organisational Studies*, Vol. 15, pp. 296-312

O'Malley M (2000), *Creating Commitment*, John Wiley & Sons. Chichester

Organ D W, Paine J B (1999), 'A new kind of performance for industrial and organizational psychology: Recent contributions to the study of organizational citizenship behavior', in Cooper C L, Robertson I T (eds), *International Review of Industrial and Organizational Psychology*, Vol. 14, pp. 337-367, London, John Wiley & Sons

Organ D W, Ryan K (1995), 'A meta-analytic review of attitudinal and dispostional predictors of organizational citizenship behaviors', *Personnel Psychology*, Vol. 48, pp. 775-802

Organ D W (1988), *Organizational Citizenship Behavior: The good soldier syndrome*, Lexington, MA: Lexington Books

Parks M, Floyd K (1996), 'Meanings for closeness and intimacy in friendship', *Journal of Social and Personal Relationships*, Vol. 13, pp. 85-107

Podsakoff P M, Mackenzie S B (1994), 'Organizational citizenship behavior and sales unit effectiveness', *Journal of Marketing Research*, Vol. 31, pp. 351-363

Podsakoff P M, MacKenzie S B, Paine J B, Bacharach D G (2000), 'Organizational citizenship behaviors: A critical review of the theoretical and empirical literature and suggestions for future research', *Journal of Management*, Vol. 26(3), pp. 513-565

Podsakoff P N, Ahearne M, MacKenzie S B (1997), 'Organizational citizenship behavior and the quantity and quality of work group performance', *Journal of Applied Psychology*, Vol. 82(2), pp. 262-270

Premack S, Wanous J (1985), 'A meta-analysis of realistic job preview experiments', *Journal of Applied Psychology*, Vol. 70, pp. 706-719

Robinson S L (1996), 'Trust and breach of the psychological contract', *Administrative Science Quarterly*, Vol. 41, pp. 574-599

Rousseau D M (1995), *Psychological Contracts in Organizations: Understanding written and unwritten agreements*, Thousand Oaks, CA, Sage Publications

Rucci A J, Kirn S, Quinn R T (1998), 'The employee-customer-profit chain at Sears', *Harvard Business Review*, Jan-Feb, pp. 83-97

Rusbult C, Buunk B (1993), 'Commitment processes in close relationships: An interdependence analysis', *Journal of Social and Personal Relationships*, Vol. 10, pp. 175-204

Schwarzwald J, Koslowsky M, Shalit B (1992), 'A field study of employees' attitudes and behaviours after promotion decisions', *Journal of Applied Psychology*, Vol. 77, pp. 511-514

Settoon R, Bennet N, Liden R, (1996), 'Social exchange in organisations: Perceived organisational support, leader-member exchange, and employee reciprocity', *Journal of Applied Psychology*, Vol. 81, pp. 219-227

Sturges J, Guest D (2000), 'Who's in charge? Graduates' attitudes to and experiences of career management and their relationship with organizational commitment'. *European Journal of Work and Organizational Psychology*, Vol. 9 (3), pp. 351-370

The Families and Work Institute (1998), Reported in *USA Today*, July, No. 43

Troy K (1998), *Managing the Corporate Brand*, The Conference Board, New York

Turnley W H, Bolino M C, Lester S W, Bloodgood J M (2003), 'The impact of psychological contract fulfilment on the performance of in-role and organizational citizenship behaviors', *Journal of Management*, Vol. 29(2), pp. 187-206

Vandenberg R, Lance C (1992), 'Satisfaction and organisational commitment,' *Journal of Management*, Vol. 18, pp. 153-167

VanYpren N W, Van Den Berg A E, Willering M C (1999), 'Towards a better understanding of the link between participation in decision-making and organizational citizenship behavior: A multilevel analysis', *Journal of Occupational and Organizational Psychology*, Vol. 73, pp. 377-392

Walker Information Inc (2000), *Employee Commitment and the Bottom Line: Ethical Issues in the Employer-Employee Relationship*, Work, USA

Wall T D, Jackson P R, Davids K (1992), Operator work design and robotics system performance: a serendipitous field study *Journal of Applied Psychology*, Vol. 77, pp. 353-362

Walton R (1985), 'From control to commitment in the workplace', *Harvard Business Review*, Vol. 63, No. 2, March-April

Wanous J P, Poland T D, Premack S L, Davis K S (1992), 'The effects of met expectations on newcomer attitudes and behaviors: A review and meta-analysis' *Journal of Applied Psychology*, Vol. 77, pp. 288-297

Williams S, Pitre R, Zainuba M (2002), 'Justice and organizational citizenship behavior intentions: Fair rewards versus fair treatment', *The Journal of Social Psychology*, Vol. 142(1), pp. 33-44

Zellars K L, Tepper B J, Duffy M K (2002), 'Abusive supervision and subordinates' organizational citizenship behavior', *Journal of Applied Psychology*, Vol. 87(6), pp. 1068-1076